Jane Eyre

Charlotte Brontë

Level 4

1300 Headwords

Retold by

C.S. Woolley

Jane Eyre
Charlotte Brontë

First published 2018
by Foxton Books
London, UK

ISBN: 978-1-911481-26-3

Retold by C.S. Woolley
Inner illustrations by Alexander Solovyov
Cover by Luibov Bodnarska

Printed by Mega Printing in Turkey

Foxton Readers are a series of carefully graded books aimed at ESL / EAL learners of beginner to advanced levels. They are based on a comprehensive grammar and vocabulary framework to match each ability level and to ensure each learner progresses. They are not only suitable for ESL / EAL learners but can also be used with native speakers of primary and secondary school age.

CONTENTS

INTRODUCTION

Jane Eyre was an orphan who lived with her aunt and cousins who were all very unkind to her.

After being sent to school to study, she became a governess to Miss Varens at Thornfield. This is where she met Mr Rochester, a lonely man with a dark secret who she fell in love with. Eventually, Jane realised she had to get away from the house and the mysteries it held. One night, she left Thornfield forever.

ABOUT THE AUTHOR

Charlotte Brontë was born on April 21, 1816 in Thornton, Yorkshire, England. She was a 19th century writer whose novel, *Jane Eyre*, is considered to be a classic of Western literature.

She was the third of six children. Her father was a clergyman. Her mother died of cancer in 1821. Her aunt Elizabeth took care of the children after their mother's death.

Charlotte Brontë had a deep interest in writing. She published her first novel, *Jane Eyre*, in 1847 under the pen name of Currer Bell. Her other novels include *Shirley* (1848) and *Villette* (1853).

She died in Haworth, Yorkshire in 1855.

Chapter 1

We couldn't go for a walk that afternoon. We had gone out for a walk in the morning, but the cold winter wind had brought heavy rain so we couldn't go outside. I was very happy to stay inside. I didn't like going for long walks.

Eliza, John and Georgina were all sitting around their mother. She was lying on the sofa by the fire. I was in trouble. Bessie, the nurse, had said something to their mother. I was sent into the breakfast room next door. I sat down and read a book. I liked reading books. I even liked listening to Bessie reading books when she was in a good mood.

I sat in the window seat and drew the curtain. John Reed came looking for me.

"What were you doing behind the curtain?" he asked.

"I was reading," I replied.

"You are a servant. You can't read our books. I am going to teach you a lesson," John said. He picked up the book and threw it at me. It hit me and I fell over. I cut my head. Mrs. Reed came into the room.

"Take her away to the red room and lock her in there," she said. Bessie and the maid dragged me away. I tried to get free but I couldn't. They took me to the red room and made me sit on a **stool**.

stool (n) a seat without back or arms

He picked up the book and threw it at me.
It hit me and I fell over.

"If you don't **sit still**, we will tie you up," Bessie said.

"You know that you will have to go to the poorhouse if Mrs. Reed sends you away," Bessie said, "You aren't equal to the family. Mrs. Reed was kind when she let you be **brought up** with her children. You need to learn your place."

Bessie and the maid left the red room and locked the door. The red room was a bedroom that was only used when lots of people visited Gateshead Hall. The room was very cold because the fire wasn't lit.

Mr. Reed had died in the red room. No one came into the room unless Mrs. Reed said so. It made a very good prison. I sat and thought about my life. Why was I always suffering? Why could I never do anything to make Mrs. Reed happy? Eliza was **selfish**. Georgia was spoiled and horrible. John was nasty and broke the necks of pigeons, killed peachicks and set the dogs on the sheep.

My head hurt and it was still bleeding. No one had asked me about my head or told John off. I made up my mind to run away. If I couldn't run away, then I would stop drinking and eating and die.

sit still (idiom) to sit without moving around
bring up (phrasal verb) to take care of a child and teach him or her how to behave
selfish (adj) if you are selfish, you care only for yourself, not others

I was Mr. Reed's niece. If he were alive, I knew he would have been nice to me. I started crying. Then I saw a light in the room. I thought it was a ghost. I screamed. I ran to the door and tried to pull it open.

Bessie and the maid opened the door.

"Are you ill?" Bessie asked.

"Let me out. I want to go to the nursery," I cried.

"What is wrong?" Bessie asked.

"I saw a light. I thought it was a ghost," I cried.

"She is lying," the maid said.

"What is going on?" Mrs. Reed came along the corridor.

"Miss Jane screamed," the maid said.

"Go back in the room. Nothing is wrong with her. She is a liar," Mrs. Reed **snarled**. I was still crying. Mrs. Reed was very angry. She pushed me back in the room and locked the door again.

I woke up on the bed. Bessie and a strange man stood next to the bed. The man was Mr. Lloyd. He was a doctor. Bessie gave me some water.

"Bessie, am I ill?" I asked.

snarl (v) to speak in an angry way

"Yes. You will be better soon," Bessie said. Mr. Lloyd left. I was in the nursery. Bessie went into the next room. I heard her say, "Sarah, come and sit with me tonight. Miss Jane might die. I don't want to be on my own."

I fell asleep. When I woke up, I felt terrible and I cried. Bessie brought me some food and a book to read. Mr. Lloyd came to see me again.

"What made you ill yesterday?" he asked.

"She had a fall," Bessie said.

"Fall?" Mr Lloyd asked.

"I was knocked down," I said. Mr. Lloyd sent Bessie away.

"What made you ill?" he asked.

"I was locked in a room with a ghost," I said.

"You are afraid of ghosts?" Mr. Lloyd asked.

"Only of Mr. Reed's ghost. He died in that room," I said.

"Are you scared now?" Mr. Lloyd asked.

"No, but I am unhappy," I replied.

"Why?" he asked.

"John Reed **knocked me down** and my aunt locked me up. I have to leave and live somewhere else," I said.

knock someone down (phrasal verb) to hit someone and make them fall

"Do you have other relatives?" Mr. Lloyd asked.

"No," I said.

"Would you like to go to school?" he asked.

"Yes," I said.

Mr. Lloyd went to find Mrs. Reed.

I didn't hear anything else from Mr. Lloyd. I got better slowly. I stayed in the nursery, away from the family. Three months went by. Christmas came and went. One day, Bessie came to get me. She was in a big hurry. She took me to see Mrs. Reed. There was a man with her.

"How old is she?" the man asked.

"Ten years old," Mrs. Reed said.

"What is your name?" the man asked.

"Jane Eyre," I said.

"Mr. Brocklehurst, will you take her to Lowood School or not?" Mrs. Reed asked.

"I will. I will write to Miss Temple too and tell her a new girl is coming," said Mr. Brocklehurst and left the room.

"Go back to the nursery, Jane," Mrs. Reed ordered.

"I hate you and your children. John is mean and Georgina lies. I will never call you aunt again. I will tell everyone how horrible you have been to me," I said.

"How dare you!" Mrs. Reed shouted.

"It is the truth! I will remember how horrible you have been to me. You lie to everyone," I replied. I felt free. Mrs. Reed looked scared.

"Do you want some water?" Mrs. Reed asked.

"No," I said.

"Is there anything you want? I want to be your friend Jane," Mrs. Reed said.

"I don't want anything except to go to school," I said. Mrs. Reed **nodded**, got up and left me on my own. I sat down and started to read a book.

"Miss Jane, where are you? Come to lunch," Bessie called. She came to find me.

"I don't feel like coming to lunch," I said.

"What is it?" Bessie asked.

"Everyone hates me in this house," I said.

"That's not true. I love you more than the others," Bessie said.

"You don't show it," I replied.

"What makes you say things like that?" Bessie asked.

nod (v) to move your head up and down as a way of showing agreement, understanding or approval

"I am going away soon. I didn't want to keep quiet about how I feel," I said.

"Are you glad that you are leaving?" Bessie asked.

"No. I was until I spoke to you," I said.

"If I asked you for a kiss, you wouldn't give me one. You would tell me no!" Bessie told me.

"I will give you a kiss," I said. Bessie bent down and I hugged her. I kissed her cheek and I felt better than I ever had before. The afternoon was lovely. I felt very calm and **peaceful**. Bessie told me stories and sang songs to me. I was happy. Even my life had some happy moments of sunshine.

Bessie bent down and I hugged her.
I kissed her cheek.

peaceful (adj) quiet and calm, not liking violence; pleasant

Chapter 2

I left Gateshead at 6 a.m. on 19th January. I only said goodbye to Bessie. It was very dark when I left. Lowood School was fifty miles away from Gateshead. It was still dark when I got there. I was taken into the school by a lady called Miss Miller. There was a tall lady with dark hair. She was sitting in the room. Her name was Miss Temple.

"Are you tired?" she asked me.

"A little," I replied.

"And hungry? Give her some supper before bed, Miss Miller. Is this the first time you have left your parents to come to school?" the tall woman asked.

I told her I didn't have any parents. We talked about my life and then she sent me to bed. She was a very kind lady. Miss Miller **led** me through the school to a room that had other girls in. The older girls brought out supper for everyone to eat. Miss Miller said prayers and then everyone went to bed. Miss Miller took me to a bed in a room that had two rows of beds in it.

lead (v) to show the way to someone

It was cold when I woke up. I got dressed and a bell rang to start school. All the girls went down to a different room and got into separate groups. These were the classes. They put me at the bottom of the lowest class.

We had lessons for an hour and then had breakfast. It was burnt porridge. No one ate any because burnt porridge is horrible. We all went back to lessons.

Miss Temple came into the room. When it was close to lunch time, she spoke, "I know that breakfast was horrible this morning. I have ordered a special lunch of bread and cheese for everyone," she said. Everyone seemed surprised.

We all ate lunch. It was very tasty. Then we went outside. No one had spoken to me yet. I felt very lonely. I saw a girl reading a book so I went over to talk to her.

"Is your book interesting?" I asked.

"I like it," she **replied**.

"What is it about?" I asked.

"You can look at it, if you want," she said and handed the book to me. I looked at it. The book was called *Rasselas*. I thought it looked very boring. It didn't have any fairies in it. I gave it back to her and she started reading again.

reply (v) to answer

I saw a girl reading a book so I went over to talk to her. "Is your book interesting?" I asked.

"Why does it say that the school is an institution on the sign over there?" I asked.

"Because it is a **charity** school. I guess that you are an orphan," she replied.

"Both of my parents died before I can remember," I said.

"We are all orphans," she told me.

I learned that Miss Temple was the Superintendent of the school and Mr. Brocklehurst was **in charge of** it. He didn't live at the school but he did live nearby. He was a **clergyman** and bought all the food and clothes for the girls at the school. The girl got bored of my questions and went back to reading.

Then it was time for dinner. After dinner, we had more lessons. We had tea at 5 p.m. After tea, it was time to study. Then we had supper and went to bed. That was my first day at Lowood.

Every day at Lowood was the same. Some of the teachers were strict. I thought they were cruel. The other girls said that they were not.

charity (n) an institution or organisation that helps people in need
in charge of (phrase) responsible for, being in control of
clergyman (n) a male priest

The girl who was reading *Rasselas* was called Helen Burns. She told me about the teachers and which were easy to learn from and which teachers were hard to learn from. When Helen listened to lessons by Miss Temple, she always paid attention.

On Sundays, we walked to Mr. Brocklehurst's church. At the end of the service, we all walked back. When we got home, we listened to Miss Miller who was reading a **sermon**.

Mr. Brocklehurst came to visit Lowood School several times. When he came to the school, he spent his time watching us work and talking to Miss Temple. He told Miss Temple off for giving us bread and cheese when we couldn't eat breakfast. He wanted us to be strong young women who suffered like Jesus. He ordered Miss Temple to cut off the hair of all the girls with curly hair. He thought that curled hair wasn't natural and was a luxury. We weren't allowed anything that might be a luxury. When he was finished with the girls with curly hair, he ordered all the girls with braided hair and top knots to have theirs cut off too.

Mr. Brocklehurst was a horrible man. He saw me and made me sit on a stool in the middle of the room. He told everyone that I was evil and a liar. He told everyone to never talk to me. When he was gone, I went to the corner. I sat down and cried. I had worked hard and was at the top of my class.

sermon (n) a speech about a religious subject or a moral topic

It didn't matter what I did. People always hated me. Helen Burns brought me coffee and bread at tea time.

"Don't worry, nobody believes Mr. Brocklehurst," she said. Helen hugged me and made me feel better. Miss Temple came to find us and took us to her office.

She gave us cups of tea in china cups and something to eat. She asked me about my aunt and what she was like. I told her about my aunt. Miss Temple kissed my **forehead** when I finished. She asked Helen about her chest which sometimes made her ill. The housekeeper had refused to send extra bread and butter up, but Miss Temple had a seed cake that she gave to us.

We sat beside the fire and I listened to Miss Temple and Helen talk. Miss Temple was clever as well as beautiful. Helen was clever too. They talked about lots of things – books, history and secrets of nature. When it was time for us to go to bed, she hugged us both.

A week later, a letter arrived from Mr. Lloyd. Miss Temple read it to all the teachers. It told them all how Mrs. Reed had lied and that Mr. Brocklehurst was wrong about me. All the teachers shook hands with me and kissed me. It made all the other girls happy.

forehead (n) the part of the face above the eyes

I felt so good that I worked even harder than before. I was moved to a harder class and started to learn French and how to draw. I now loved living at Lowood and wanted to stay there forever. I never wanted to go back to Gateshead.

Lowood was very pretty in the summer. It had lots of trees and flowers and it was a nice place to go walking but I had to go walking alone. More than half of the girls became sick so the bedroom was turned into a hospital.

Miss Temple looked after all the sick girls. The girls who weren't ill had to do lots of exercise to stay healthy. Some of the girls were sent to their relatives' homes to die. Some of them died at the school and were buried very quickly. Mr. Brocklehurst stayed away from Lowood while everyone was sick. The housekeeper ran away because she didn't want to get sick. It meant that there was more food to eat and everyone who was well was much happier.

We spent our time outside whenever we could. We even ate dinner outside. Helen was sick and I had to find someone else to talk to. I came back from walking one day and saw the doctor at the school.

"Doctor, why are you here?" I asked.

"To see Helen Burns. She is very sick. She won't be here long," he told me. I didn't know that he meant that she was dying. I went to see Helen after they had sent us to bed. She was cold and thin.

I went to see Helen after they had sent us to bed.
She was cold and thin.

"Why are you here?" Helen asked.

"I had to see you," I said.

"You came to say goodbye," Helen said.

"Are you going home?" I asked.

"I am going to my last home," Helen told me.

"No! You can't," I said.

"I am happy, Jane. We all have to die. I am going to God," Helen said. I fell asleep next to Helen. When I woke up, the nurse was carrying me back to bed. Helen had died and no one **told** me **off** for being with her.

tell somebody off (phrasal verb) to speak in an angry way to someone for doing something wrong

Chapter 3

After so many girls died at the school, people started to ask questions about the school. Mr. Brocklehurst got into a lot of trouble. Lots of rich people gave money to the school so we had better clothes and food. A committee was formed to manage the school. I stayed at Lowood for six years as a pupil and then I was asked to be a teacher. Miss Temple got married and moved away. I missed her a lot and I missed Helen. I had not left Lowood since I first arrived, but it was time for me to go somewhere new.

I put an **advert** in the newspaper. I was going to be a **governess**. I went to work for Mrs. Fairfax at Thornfield. Bessie came to see me before I left Lowood. She was married and had a little boy and a girl called Jane. She told me about the family at Gateshead. I played the piano for her and gave her one of my paintings. She told me that Mr. Eyre had been to Gateshead to look for me before he went to a foreign country. He was my uncle. He was disappointed that I wasn't there. When I said goodbye to Bessie, I went to Thornfield.

advert (n) advertisement, something (e.g. picture, film) shown to people to help sell a product

governess (n) a woman who lives with a family and is paid to teach their child in their home

I was going to teach a ten year old girl called Miss Varens. When I got to Thornfield, Mrs. Fairfax was sitting by the fire. She was knitting.

"Come in, you must be cold," she said to me. I sat down by the fire and warmed my hands. Mrs. Fairfax asked the servants to bring me something hot to drink and something to eat. Mrs. Fairfax didn't have any family. She was very happy to have me living at Thornfield. I wasn't just a teacher for Miss Varens, but also a friend for Mrs. Fairfax.

My bedroom was next to Mrs. Fairfax's bedroom. It was very comfortable. I met Mrs. Fairfax the next morning. She asked me what I thought of Thornfield. I told her I liked it very much.

"It is a very pretty place. It would be perfect if Mr. Rochester came to live here and looked after it properly," Mrs. Fairfax said.

"Who is Mr. Rochester?" I asked.

"He owns Thornfield," she told me.

"I thought it was your house," I said.

"No, I am the housekeeper," she replied.

"Who is Miss Varens?" I asked.

I sat down by the fire and warmed my hands.

"She is Mr. Rochester's **ward**. He asked me to find her a governess. Here she comes now," Mrs. Fairfax said. "Good morning, Miss Varens. Come and meet Jane Eyre. She is your new governess."

Miss Varens talked in French to her nurse. They were both from France and didn't speak much English. I led Miss Varens in to breakfast and spoke to her in French. Mrs. Fairfax was **impressed** and Miss Varens was happy.

She told me about coming to England and where she had grown up in France. She told me about her mother. After breakfast, she sat on my knee and sang for me. Then she read me a poem. She told me how her mother had died and that Mr. Rochester had promised that Miss Varens could come and live with him.

"But he isn't here. He has gone back to France. I never see him," Miss Varens said.

We used the library for Miss Varens' lessons. There were lots of books to help me teach her, and books that I could read. Miss Varens had not had lessons before so we started with morning lessons. In the afternoons, I let her go outside with her nurse.

ward (n) a child who lives under the protection of a guardian

impressed (adj) if you are impressed by something, you are strongly affected by it because it is so good and interesting

Mrs. Fairfax said, "Good morning, Miss Varens. Come and meet Jane Eyre. She is your new governess."

I was going to draw, but I went to see Mrs. Fairfax instead. She told me about Mr. Rochester. I found out that Mr. Rochester was liked by the people in the neighbourhood. He would come and go without warning. He seemed to be a good man but he was different from other gentlemen. Mrs. Fairfax thought he was difficult to understand. He was a gentleman and a landowner and that was all I needed to know.

Mrs. Fairfax showed me around the house. It was a very pretty place with lots of old furniture. Most of the rooms were never used. I asked Mrs. Fairfax if there were any ghosts at Thornfield.

"No," she told me. She took me onto the roof. There was a nice view of the countryside from the top of the house. As we came down from the roof, I heard someone laugh.

"Mrs. Fairfax, did you hear someone laughing?" I asked.

"It will be one of the servants," Mrs. Fairfax said.

"Did you hear it?" I said again.

"Yes. I hear it all the time," Mrs. Fairfax said.

I heard the laugh again. It made me think of ghosts, but Mrs. Fairfax was sure that it was a servant.

"Grace! That is too much noise," Mrs. Fairfax said. The servant, Grace, came out of a room and apologised to Mrs. Fairfax. We went downstairs for dinner with Miss Varens.

I liked living at Thornfield. Mrs. Fairfax was nice. Miss Varens worked hard in her lessons and I liked her very much. Her nurse was also lovely. When Miss Varens played with her nurse, I went up to the roof and looked at the view.

I heard Grace laughing when I came up and went down. I saw her sometimes as well. I tried to talk to her but she didn't reply to me. Thornfield was near a village called Hay. Miss Varens was ill one day so I walked to the village. When I was walking, a horse came down the road. A dog ran beside it. The rider on the horse was a gentleman. The horse slipped on some ice and the horse and the rider fell to the ground. I went over to see if I could help.

"Are you okay?" I asked.

"Stand aside," the man said. The dog **leaped** at his master, "Down, Pilot," he said to the dog. The horse stood up and the man checked it for any injuries.

"Do you need me to get someone from Hay or Thornfield?" I asked.

"Thank you, I don't have any broken bones, only a **sprained** ankle," he said. He tried to put his foot on the ground and cried out in pain.

leap (v) to jump; to spring

sprain (v) to injure (e.g. ankle, knee) by twisting it in a sudden and painful way

"I can't leave you here. Let me help you," I said.

"Isn't it a bit late for you to be out on your own? Where do you live?" he asked.

"I am just going to post a letter. I live at Thornfield," I said.

"Who owns the house?" he asked.

"Mr. Rochester," I said.

"Do you know, Mr. Rochester?" he asked.

"No, I have never met him. He isn't at Thornfield," I said.

"You aren't a servant, are you?" he asked.

"I am the governess," I replied.

"I can't send you to get help, but you can help me," he said. He asked me to bring his horse over to help him walk. I led the horse over and helped him to his feet. I gave him his whip that had gone under the hedge. He set off down the road and I went to post Mrs. Fairfax's letter.

It was very dark when I got back to Thornfield. I looked at the stars and the moon before I went into the house. Pilot, Mr. Rochester's dog, was in the house. He came over and sniffed me.

"Jane! Mr. Rochester has arrived," the nurse said in French as she came down the hall.

"Is Mrs. Fairfax with him?" I asked.

"Yes and Miss Varens. The doctor is coming. His horse fell over and Mr. Rochester sprained his ankle," the nurse said.

The man I met in the lane was Mr. Rochester.

"I can't leave you here. Let me help you," I said.

Chapter 4

Mr. Rochester went to bed early. The next day people came to see him on business. He saw them in the library so Miss Varens' lessons had to be moved. We used one of the upstairs rooms instead. The house was busy and it was much nicer than it had been.

Miss Varens kept leaving the lessons to look for Mr. Rochester. I got angry and she sat still. When it was dark outside, I let Miss Varens go to find Mr. Rochester. He asked Miss Varens and me to have tea with him. I had to dress up for tea. Mrs. Fairfax got out my black silk dress and a pearl brooch that Miss Temple gave me.

I went down to the dining room. Pilot lay by the fire. Miss Varens sat on the floor by Mr. Rochester's chair. He was sitting with his foot on a stool. He wasn't paying any attention to me as I came in and sat down. Mrs. Fairfax sat down and started talking. Mr. Rochester only asked Mrs. Fairfax for tea.

Miss Varens suddenly asked Mr. Rochester to give me a present. Mr. Rochester looked at me and angrily asked, "Did you want a present, Miss Eyre? Do you like presents?"

He was sitting with his foot on a stool. He wasn't paying any attention to me as I came in and sat down.

"I don't know. Most people think they are nice things," I replied.

"I asked what you think," he said.

"I need time to think of an answer that is worthy to give you," I replied.

"Don't try to be **modest**! I know Miss Varens is not a special child, but she has learned a lot from you," he said crossly.

"That is the best present to give me. Teachers only want to hear praise for their students," I said.

Mr. Rochester didn't sound impressed. He went back to sitting in silence. After tea, Miss Varens showed me around the room.

"Come to the fire," Mr. Rochester said. I sat down and Miss Varens was told to go and play with the dog.

"Where did you come from?" Mr. Rochester asked.

"Lowood School," I replied.

"How long were you there?" he asked.

"Eight years," I said.

"What about your parents?" he asked.

"They are dead," I replied.

modest (adj) a modest person doesn't talk too much about themselves or their abilities and doesn't show or feel great pride

"Do you remember them?" he asked.

"No," I said.

"Do you have any family?" he asked

"Not that I have met," I said.

"How did you end up here?" he asked.

"I put an advert in the newspaper. Mrs. Fairfax asked me to come here," I replied. He asked me lots of questions about my life. He **teased** me about not being beautiful. He blamed me for his horse falling over. He sent me to play the piano. He was judging me. He asked me about my drawings. He wanted to see all of them. I showed them to him. He looked at three pictures I had drawn at Lowood. The first one was clouds over the sea. The second one was a hill at sunset. The third was an iceberg with the northern lights behind it.

After he had talked about the paintings, he told me to put them away and take Miss Varens to bed. Mrs. Fairfax told me that Mr. Rochester's older brother had died and he had no family. She said, "His sad thoughts make his mood change very quickly."

tease (v) to make fun of

Mr. Rochester's ankle got better. He went riding every day. When I saw him, sometimes he was nice, sometimes he was horrible. One night, he called Miss Varens and me down to tea. There was a present for Miss Varens. Mr. Rochester told me to sit with him by the fire. Miss Varens sat with Mrs. Fairfax and told the housekeeper all about her present.

Mr. Rochester looked happy. I stared at him. He caught me staring.

"Do you think I am handsome?" he asked.

"No, sir," I said. He laughed.

"Why not?" he asked. I tried to go back on my answer, but he wouldn't let me. He asked me what I thought about his character. I didn't know what to say. "You are as pretty as I am handsome, but thinking suits you. I want to know you better," he said to me.

He asked me questions and I answered them. The conversation was more like an argument. When it reached 9 p.m., I stood up to take Miss Varens to bed.

"Miss Varens isn't ready to go to bed yet. She is putting on the pink dress I bought her. She is going to come back in a minute. She is going to look just like her mother. It is going to be painful to see. Stay with me until then," Mr. Rochester said.

I didn't understand why he was upset. He told me that he had loved Miss Varens' mother. He told me about all the money he had spent on her and that he thought he was loved by her. He went to see her one night and found her with another man. He fought a **duel** against the man she was with. Celine Varens, Miss Varens' mother, said that Miss Varens was Mr. Rochester's daughter and he had left her to run away to Italy.

After he had finished telling me the story, he said, "In a few days, you will come and tell me that you have found somewhere new to work and that you don't want to teach a girl who was **abandoned** by her mother."

"Not at all. I like Miss Varens. I will not abandon her," I said. The more time I spent with Mr. Rochester, the more I liked him. I even thought he was handsome.

One day, eight weeks after Mr. Rochester had arrived, I went to bed and heard a strange noise. It came from above me. I was scared. I couldn't sleep. I heard a horrible laugh outside my door.

"Who is there?" I cried. I heard steps outside my door. I got out of bed to go to Mrs. Fairfax. Outside my door, the corridor was full of smoke. It smelled like something was on fire. The smoke and smell both came from Mr. Rochester's room.

duel (n) a fight between two people
abandon (v) to leave and never come back to someone/something

I ran to Mr. Rochester's room. I opened the door. Mr. Rochester was asleep on his bed and the room was on fire. I tried to wake him up. When I couldn't, I **put out** the fire with jugs of water. The water woke up Mr. Rochester. I told him what had happened. He told me to sit down in his chair. He gave me his **cloak** to keep warm.

Mr. Rochester went to check the house. When he came back he said, "Don't say anything about this to anyone. You should go to bed. I will sleep in the library."

"Good night," I said.

"Wait, thank you for saving my life," he told me. He looked like he was going to say something else but he stopped himself.

"I am glad I was awake," I replied. He held my hands for a long time. Eventually, I went to bed. I was **confused** about Mr. Rochester. The next day, he went to the Leas for a party. He wasn't coming back for at least a week.

I was very upset. I thought he loved me, but I was wrong. I sat down with a mirror and drew my portrait. I wasn't pretty. I called it *Portrait of a Governess*.

put out (phrasal verb) to extinguish; to cause (e.g. fire) to stop burning
cloak (n) a piece of clothing used as a coat
confused (adj) unable to understand or think clearly

He held my hands for a long time.

Chapter 5

Mr. Rochester was away for three weeks. When he came back, he brought lots of people with him. The first night, Mr. Rochester held a party but I was not invited.

The next day, the party went out. I gave Miss Varens her lessons. Mrs. Fairfax told me, "Mr. Rochester wants Miss Varens to meet everyone and you to go with her," she said. She told me how to behave in front of all the ladies and gentlemen. I put on the dress I wore to Miss Temple's wedding and Miss Varens wore her pink dress. I also wore my pearl brooch.

We waited in the drawing room for everyone to finish dinner. Eight ladies came in and **whisked** Miss Varens away from me to sit on the sofa. I sat by the wall and waited. The gentlemen came in with the coffee. Mr Rochester didn't look at me. He sat down on the opposite side of the room with the ladies.

I now knew that I was in love with him. The party talked about Miss Varens and governesses. None of them liked governesses. One of the ladies sat and played the piano while Mr. Rochester sang.

When he had finished singing, I left the room. Mr. Rochester followed me.

whisk (v) to move someone or something to another place very quickly

When he had finished singing, I left the room.
Mr. Rochester followed me.

"How do you do?" he asked.

"I am well," I said.

"Why didn't you come and talk to me?" he asked.

"I didn't want to be in your way," I replied.

"What have you done since I left?" he asked.

"I have taught Miss Varens her lessons," I said.

"You look sick. What is the matter?" he asked.

"Nothing, sir," I replied.

"Did you get sick when you put out the fire?" he asked.

"No," I said.

"Then go back to the drawing room. You can't abandon me so early," he said.

"I am tired," I said. He looked at me for a minute.

"You are upset. What is it? Tell me," he said.

"Nothing. I am not upset," I said.

"Yes, you are. You are about to cry. I won't ask you to tell me now, but I want you to come to the drawing room every night my friends are here. Send the nurse to get Miss Varens. Good night," he said.

A new gentleman came to the house. His name was Mr. Mason. The girls thought he was pretty. I didn't like him.

A **fortune teller** came to the house to read the fortunes of the young ladies. The young ladies were Blanche Ingram, her sister, Mary Ingram, and Amy and Louisa Eshton. Blanch Ingram wanted to marry Mr. Rochester. She was a nasty woman who was horrible to Miss Varens. Blanche went to see the fortune teller first.

When she came back, she told everyone that the woman was a liar and a fake. Mary, Amy and Louisa went to see the fortune teller together. They were too scared to go alone. The three girls believed that she was a real fortune teller.

The servant came over to me and said the fortune teller wanted to see me. I went into the room and sat down. The fortune teller asked, "Why don't you **tremble**?"

"I'm not cold," I said.

"Why don't you turn pale?" she asked.

"I am not sick," I said.

"Why don't you ask me questions?" she asked.

"I am not silly," I replied. She laughed at me.

fortune teller (n) someone who tells you what will happen to you in the future
tremble (v) to shake

"You are cold. You are sick and you are silly," she told me.

"Prove it," I said.

"You are cold because you are alone. You are sick because the best feelings stay away from you. You are silly because you suffer without needing too," she told me. "Show me your palm. I will read it."

I gave her a shilling and she looked at my hand and then she looked at my forehead. She spoke in riddles. When she had finished, I saw her hand and knew who the woman was, and, "You are not a fortune teller," I said.

"You know me?" he asked.

"Take off the red cloak," I said.

"The string is **in a knot**. Help me," he said.

"Break it," I said. Mr. Rochester broke the string and took off the cloak.

"What a strange thing to do," I told him.

"Yes, but it **came off well**," he replied.

"With the ladies," I said.

"Do you forgive me, Jane?" he asked.

come off well (idiom) to be successful; to have a good result in a competition, fight, etc.

in a knot (phrase) twisted together (e.g. hair, string, shoelaces)

"You are not a fortune teller," I said.
"You know me?" he asked.
"Take off the red cloak," I said.

"I may, but it was not right for you to do," I replied.

"You are right. What is everyone doing in the drawing room?" he asked.

"Talking about the fortune teller. Did you know a man called Mr. Mason arrived today?" I asked.

"Mason!" he went pale. He **gripped** my wrist.

"What is wrong?" I asked.

"Jane, I need your support," he said.

"You have it," I replied. We sat down. He held both my hands.

"I wish the two of us were living on an island far away from here. Somewhere trouble couldn't reach us," he said.

"Can I help? I will do anything to help you," I told him.

"I need a glass of wine. If you see Mason, tell me what he is doing," he said. I did what Mr. Rochester asked. I told him that they were all laughing and talking.

"What would you do if everyone **turned against** me?" he asked.

"I would stay with you," I said.

"To comfort me?" he asked.

"Yes," I said.

grip (v) to hold something tightly
turn against (phrasal verb) to stop being friendly to someone, to be their enemy

"Go to Mr. Mason, **whisper** in his ear that I am in the library and want to talk to him," he told me.

"Yes, sir," I said. I took Mr. Mason to Mr. Rochester and then I went to bed.

I woke up. I had forgotten to close my curtains and the moonlight woke me. I went to close my curtains when there was a horrible cry. It rang through the house. I was very scared. It came from above me.

"Help, help, help! Will no one come?" a voice cried, "Rochester, for God's sake, help!"

I heard a door open and footsteps. I got dressed and went to see what was going on. Everyone was out of bed and in the corridor.

"What is going on?" Blanche asked. Mr Rochester came down from the floor above.

"A servant had a nightmare. Go back to bed. Nothing is wrong," he said. I went back to my room and sat by the window. I waited to see if anything else would happen.

When the house was quiet, there was a knock at my door.

"Yes?" I said.

"Are you up and dressed?" Mr. Rochester asked.

whisper (v) to speak very softly or quietly

"Come out quietly. I want to show you something," he said. I did what he asked. He took me upstairs. He unlocked the door of the room above mine. He held my hand. We went into the room. I heard the horrible laugh.

He took me to the bed. Mr. Mason sat in a chair next to the bed. He was covered in blood and looked dead. Mr. Rochester gave me a bowl of water to hold and used smelling salts to wake Mr. Mason up.

"Am I dying?" Mr. Mason asked.

"No, you will be fine. Jane," Mr. Rochester said.

"Yes?" I replied.

"I need you to look after Mr. Mason while I go to get the doctor. Mr. Mason, if you talk to Jane, I will kill you," Mr. Rochester said. He left and locked the door. I was scared, but I did what Mr. Rochester said. I wondered what had happened to Mr. Mason and why Mr. Rochester had been scared when he arrived.

It was getting light outside when Mr. Rochester came back. The doctor was with him. He took care of Mr. Mason. Mr. Rochester sent me to get a shirt and a tie for Mr. Mason from Mr. Rochester's room. I didn't understand what was going on. A woman had attacked Mr. Mason. He had teeth marks and cuts from a knife on him.

When I gave Mr. Rochester the shirt and tie, he sent me to get Mr. Mason's cloak. The doctor and Mr. Rochester got Mr. Mason ready to leave. I went down the stairs to check for anyone walking around. The doctor and Mr. Rochester carried Mr. Mason down to a carriage. The doctor took Mr. Mason back to his house to help him get better.

Chapter 6

Bessie's husband came to Thornfield. He brought bad news.

"John Reed is dead," he said. "Mrs. Reed is very sick and wants you to come and see her."

I went to look for Mr. Rochester to ask if I could go and see Mrs. Reed. I told him about Mrs. Reed and the rest of my family. He was surprised.

"I thought you didn't have any family," he said.

"They don't want me. I am an orphan," I told him. I told Mr. Rochester that John was dead. He made me promise that I would come back to Thornfield. We talked about his marriage to Blanche and sending Miss Varens to school. I told him, "I will have to put a new advert in the newspaper for work."

Mr. Rochester made me promise not to. We said goodbye. I went to pack.

The next morning, I went to Gateshead. Bessie was waiting for me. She took me to see Mrs. Reed.

Mrs. Reed was very sick. She told me to stay for two weeks. She wanted to talk to me but she couldn't remember what she wanted to say. She forgot who I was and started talking.

"I told everyone Jane Eyre died. She didn't die but I wish she had," she said.

"Why do you hate her?" I asked.

"Her mother. My husband loved his sister and she married a poor man. When she died, my husband sent for the baby – Jane Eyre. He treated her like she was his own daughter. I hated her the moment I saw her. My husband tried to make my children treat Jane Eyre like a sister. When he died, he made me promise to look after her," Mrs. Reed said. Then she talked about John. She thought he was still alive. I got up to leave.

"Wait! He threatens me. I dream about him. He has a cut in his throat and a black face," Mrs. Reed cried. Bessie calmed Mrs. Reed and I left the room. I waited for ten days before I went to see her again. I spent my time drawing. I felt like drawing a face. I drew one without thinking. I drew Mr. Rochester. Georgina and Eliza asked me to draw their pictures. They were nice to me now but they didn't talk to each other.

Georgina wanted to go to parties. Eliza wanted to go to church. When I went to see Mrs. Reed again, she said, "I am sorry. I was horrible to you. I broke two promises. I didn't bring you up like my own daughter. The other is – go to the table, there is a letter for you."

I went to the table and read the letter there. It was from Mr. Eyre, my uncle who Bessie had told me about. He wanted to adopt me and leave me all his money. The letter was three years old.

"I told him you were dead. But you can tell him I lied and what I was like to you," Mrs. Reed said.

Mrs. Reed died in the night. I stayed at Gateshead for the funeral, helped Georgina and Eliza and then I went back to Thornfield. Georgina married a rich man and Eliza became a nun. I was happy to get back to Thornfield.

I walked back to Thornfield from Hay.

"Thank you, Mr. Rochester. I am glad to see you again. Wherever you are is my home," I said. Everyone at Thornfield was happy to see me.

It was summer. The gardens of Thornfield were very pretty in the summer. I walked in the garden with Mr. Rochester.

I walked in the garden with Mr. Rochester.

"You like Thornfield and Miss Varens, don't you?" he asked.

"Yes, sir," I said.

"And you don't want to leave either of them?" he asked.

"No," I said.

"Life is horrible. You must leave them both," he said.

"Why?" I asked.

"Miss Varens must go to school. You must find a new job," he said.

"I see," I said.

"I have found you one in Ireland. You will like it there," he said. He was sending me away from him. I would never see him again.

"I understand why I must go," I replied.

"No, you must stay," he told me.

"No, you said I must go. I must go. Do you think I can stay and be nothing to you?" I replied. Mr. Rochester hugged me. I was happy but I had to get away from him. I struggled free.

"Marry me, Jane," he said.

Mr. Rochester hugged me.
I was happy but I had to get away from him.

I thought he was teasing me.

"You think I am teasing you?" he asked.

"Yes," I said.

"Call me Edward. Say that you will marry me," he said and added, "It is **torture** to not have an answer."

"Do you really love me?" I asked.

"Yes," he said.

"Then I will be your wife, Edward," I said.

"Are you happy, Jane?" he asked.

"I am," I replied. It began to rain. We ran back to the house. Mrs. Fairfax was waiting in the hall. She watched Mr. Rochester kiss me. He went to bed. I ran upstairs to my room.

The next day, Mrs. Fairfax looked sad but I didn't know why. Mr. Rochester greeted me with a kiss.

"You will be Jane Rochester in a month," he told me. I was very happy. "The family jewels are coming here from London. You will go and get new dresses today. I will take you to Europe and show you everything," he told me.

"Why did you want me to think that you were going to marry Blanche?" I asked.

torture (n) something that gives you pain

"I wanted to make you love me," he said.

He told Mrs. Fairfax we were getting married. She was very surprised. She told me to be careful, but she was happy for me.

We went to Hay to get new dresses. I didn't want to go. Miss Varens begged to come with us. Mr. Rochester said no, but I asked him to change his mind. He told Miss Varens she was going away to school without me. Miss Varens didn't understand why. He teased her. He told her we were going to live on the moon.

I wanted to stay as Miss Varens' governess until I was married. Mr. Rochester asked me to eat dinner with him every night. We teased each other and I fell more in love with him. The month went by. Mr. Rochester became my whole world. I loved him more than anything else.

He wanted to show the world how beautiful he thought I was. I wanted to stay the plain Jane Eyre I knew I was.

Chapter 7

The month had **gone by** very quickly. Everything was ready. After the wedding, we were going away to Europe. Miss Varens was going to school. I had terrible nightmares. One was that Mr. Rochester was taken far away from me. Another was that Thornfield was nothing more than ruins. The night before, I had gone to bed and woken up to a horrible monster leaning over me.

She had long hair, horrible eyes and black skin. My wedding **veil** was torn in half and lying on the floor. When I woke up the next morning, I thought I had been dreaming but the veil was lying on the floor. I thought it must have been Grace. I was sure that she had set fire to Mr. Rochester's bedroom and hurt Mr. Mason.

I told Mr. Rochester about my dreams and about the veil. It was the night before our wedding. I had promised to sit and talk to him the night before our wedding. He was scared when I told him about the veil. He promised to tell me everything in a year and a day. He made me promise to sleep in Miss Varens' bed that night and lock the door.

The next morning, I put on my wedding dress. Mr. Rochester and I went to the church together. There were two men who were waiting at the church. We didn't have any guests. Before the wedding was over, one of the men stopped the **vicar**.

go by (phrasal verb) to pass (time)
veil (n) a piece of cloth that women wear to cover their head and shoulders
vicar (n) a priest

The next morning, I put on my wedding dress.
Mr. Rochester and I went to the church together.

"Mr. Rochester already has a wife. Her name is Betha Mason," one of the two men said. He was a lawyer. The other man was Mr. Mason. Mr. Rochester was very angry.

"She is alive and living at Thornfield. I am her brother. I saw her. She attacked me," Mr. Mason said.

"Only Mr. Rochester and his servants live there. You are lying," said the vicar.

"No, it is true. All of you come to the house. You can see her. She is a witch and mad, like the rest of her family. Jane knew nothing of this," Mr. Rochester said to the three men. We went back to Thornfield. Mr. Rochester shouted at everyone. He was upset and angry.

We went up to the room that was always locked. Mr. Rochester opened the door. Grace was cooking on the fire. But there was someone else in the room, or rather something else. In the corner, a monster ran from one wall to the other. It growled and howled.

"Good morning, Grace," Mr. Rochester said.

"Good morning, sir. Please be careful," Grace replied. I looked at the monster. It was the same monster who tore my veil. The monster was Mrs. Bertha Rochester. She attacked Mr. Rochester. She tried to kill him. When Mr. Rochester had fought her off, he sent us away. He stayed with his wife.

The lawyer spoke to me, "You are not to blame. Mr. Mason will tell your uncle about it when he goes home." They told me that Mr. Mason knew Mr. Eyre and that the letter about my wedding to Mr. Rochester made Mr. Mason come to Thornfield. Mr. Eyre was very sick and had sent Mr. Mason to save me from Mr. Rochester. Then they left Thornfield. Mr. Mason was scared of Mr. Rochester.

I went to my room and took off the wedding dress. I locked my door. I wasn't going to be Mrs. Rochester. I wanted to die. I lay on my bed and made a plan. I had to leave Thornfield. I got up and opened the door. Mr. Rochester was sitting outside it.

"You came out at last," he said. "I waited for you to **yell** at me. I was ready for it. I didn't mean to hurt you. I love you. Will you forgive me?" he asked.

"Yes. I don't want to talk. I need water," I said. Mr. Rochester picked me up and carried me downstairs. I ate and drank. Mr Rochester took care of me. He tried to kiss me. I didn't let him.

"I must leave," I told him.

"We both will. I will close the house. I will pay Grace and Mrs. Fairfax to stay here with my wife. We will go somewhere else," he said. I held his hand and cried. He told me about his wife and how she had hated and used him. He told me how I had brought him back to life.

yell (v) to shout loudly because you are angry

"I love you," I said, "but that is the last time I can say it. I must leave you."

"For how long?" he asked.

"For the rest of my life," I replied. I kissed his cheek and left him.

"If you leave me, I will have nothing. I will have no happiness. You are everything to me. Please don't go. Stay and tell me you love me. I need you. We will go away somewhere and you will be Mrs. Rochester," Mr. Rochester cried.

"Farewell forever," I said. I wanted to stay, but I knew I had to leave.

I packed my things and said goodbye to Miss Varens, Mrs. Fairfax and the nurse. I left Thornfield. I walked down the road and took a carriage as far away as I could. I slept by the road. I had nothing. I begged at a village for food and work. No one helped me. The vicar was away.

I found a farm that night. I begged the farmer for a piece of bread. He gave me some. I slept in the forest. It rained. I was not safe. I kept walking and begging. I walked onto a **moor**. It was still raining. I saw a light and walked towards it. It was a house.

moor (n) an open area of land that is not good for farming

She gave me the bread and a penny and tried to send me away.

An old woman lived there with two young ladies. I watched them for a while, then I knocked on the door. The old woman opened it. I asked her if I could have some bread and somewhere to sleep for the night.

She gave me the bread and a penny and tried to send me away. I begged her to let me in. She closed the door.

"Open the door," a man said.

"Is that you, Mr. St. John Rivers?" the old woman asked.

"Yes, let me in and bring this girl in too," he said. He took me into the house and the two young ladies, his sisters, took care of me.

I told them my name was Jane Elliot. I didn't want Mr. Rochester to find me. He might have come looking for me. They asked me where I had come from and what had happened. I couldn't answer them.

"Then what do you want from us?" Mr. St. John Rivers asked.

"Nothing," I said.

"You mean that now you have had a little food and a drink, we can throw you out into the rain on the moor?" Diana Rivers asked.

"Yes," I said. The old woman was told to come and look after me. Mr. St. John Rivers and his sisters left the room to talk about me.

I was very tired and cold. I felt better thanks to the bread and milk they had given me. I sat and waited for them to send me away. The old woman sat with me and gave me more milk.

Mary came back to the room and spoke to the old woman. When I had finished my milk, the old woman took me up the stairs, took my wet clothes and gave me a warm bed to sleep in. I went to sleep and thanked God for protecting me. I was so tired that I soon fell asleep.

Chapter 8

I was asleep for three days. Mr. St. John Rivers and his sisters let me sleep. The old woman didn't want me in the house. I wasn't sick, but I was very tired. Diana and Mary wanted to keep me. Mr. Rivers said, "She is a young lady; she probably had a **falling-out** with her friends and left. We will help her get back to them."

On the fourth day, I got out of bed and ate. My clothes had been cleaned and dried. Even my shoes had been polished. I washed my face and got dressed. I went downstairs and the old woman smiled at me.

"You are up? You must be better then," she said to me. She told me to sit down and asked, "Did you go begging before you came here?"

"I am not a beggar," I said.

"You didn't go to school," she said to me.

"I went to school for eight years," I replied. I asked the old woman about the family. Mr. St. John was the vicar in the village I went to, and the father of the family had died three weeks ago. I helped her make pies and she talked about her life.

falling-out (n) a serious argument, a quarrel

The house was called Marsh End. Diana and Mary Rivers were both going to be governesses. They had all gone out for a walk. They would be back for dinner. When they came back, Diana and Mary took me to the **parlour** and sat me down. Mr. St. John was reading a book. He was a very handsome man.

He asked me where my friends were so he could write to them and send me home.

"I don't have a home or friends," I said.

"How old are you?" he asked.

"I am nineteen," I replied. He looked at my hands to see if I was married. I went red. I thought about Mr. Rochester.

"Where did you live before you came here?" he asked.

"I am sorry. It is a secret," I replied.

"A secret that is hers to keep," Diana said.

"I can't help you if I don't know about your history. Do you need help?" Mr. St. John said.

"Yes. I need help finding a job. I don't need much money," I said.

"I will help you find a job. Tell me what you can do," he said. I had something to eat. I told Mr. St. John Rivers about my life until Thornfield. I told him that I was a governess but had to leave there eight days ago. I told him what happened when I got out of the carriage until I came to Marsh End. When I finished, I was sent to bed to rest.

parlour (n) a room for guests (reception, lounge, waiting room)

Mr. St. John was reading a book.
He was a very handsome man.

I liked the people at Marsh End. They were kind and good friends. We liked the same books and talked for hours. Diana and Mary wanted me to stay forever. Diana taught me to speak German. I taught Mary to draw.

A month had gone by. Mr. St. John Rivers hadn't said anything about work to me. Mary and Diana were going to houses in the south to be governesses in three days. I asked Mr. St. John Rivers about a job.

"I have a job for you. I want you to teach at a school for girls. I have started it. You will have a home and teach the girls from the village," he said.

"Thank you. That is wonderful," I said. I had dreamed of having my own school. We agreed that it would open next week.

The first day of school was hard. The girls were nothing like Miss Varens. When the day was over, I stood and looked at the garden. I thought about Mr. Rochester. I started to cry. Mr. St. John Rivers saw me. He had brought me a gift from his sisters. He saw I was crying. He gave me a lesson on bearing my burden.

Miss Oliver came to the school to meet me. She was beautiful and lived at the big house in the village. Mr. St. John Rivers looked at the ground. Miss Oliver asked me lots of questions. She took Mr. St. John Rivers away to see her father. He was very sick. I thought that Mr St. John Rivers was in love with Miss Oliver.

The school days got easier. The girls were all lovely. I was surprised how well they all did in their lessons. The people in the village all liked me. I liked living there. I was very happy. I still dreamed of Mr. Rochester. I dreamed I was with him and he loved me. Miss Oliver kept coming to visit me. She came to the school every day when Mr. St. John Rivers was giving one of the lessons. She came to my home and talked to me. I liked her almost as much as I liked Miss Varens.

Miss Oliver asked me to draw her for her father. It took two days to draw the picture. On the second day, Mr. Oliver came with her to meet me. He invited me to his home. I listened to him talk. He wanted Miss Oliver and Mr. St. John Rivers to get married, but Mr. St. John Rivers wanted to be a missionary. He asked me about the school and said, "I am worried that you will find somewhere else to teach. You are too good for a village school."

During the school holiday, I drew a small portrait of Miss Oliver. Mr. St. John brought me a book to read. He saw the picture. I talked to him about Miss Oliver. He told me that he loved her, but that she was not a good wife for him.

*During the school holiday,
I drew a small portrait of Miss Oliver.*

I was sure that this was not true. I told him how he changed when she was around and how she loved him. But Mr. John St. Rivers argued against marrying her. She was not a missionary's wife. He looked at the portrait several times. I asked him, "Would you like me to paint you a copy?"

"Thank you, but no. It is not wise," he said. He pulled a blank piece of paper over the portrait. Something on the blank piece of paper caught his eye. He looked at it, then looked at me. He looked back at the piece of paper and tore part of it off.

He got up, put the piece of paper in his pocket and left. I didn't know what he saw to make him act so strangely. The paper had some spots of paint on it but nothing else. I soon forgot that he had taken the scrap of paper with him.

Chapter 9

It started snowing after Mr. St John Rivers left. It snowed all night and all the next day. Mr. St. John Rivers came to see me the next night. He was covered in snow when he knocked at the door. I let him in and sat him by the fire. He didn't say anything for a while. He took a letter out of his pocket and read it.

"Twenty years ago, a poor vicar fell in love with the daughter of a rich man," Mr. St. John said. "They got married. Her family threw her out. Two years later they were both dead. They had a daughter. She was sent to live with Mr Reed at Gateshead. When she was ten, she went to Lowood School. She became a teacher. She went to Thornfield to work for Mr. Rochester."

"Mr. Rivers!" I cried.

"I know, but let me finish. Mr. Rochester asked to marry the girl. But he was already married. The girl ran away from Thornfield. People have been looking everywhere for her. A lawyer put an advert in the paper to find her. He has news for her. It is a strange story, isn't it?" he said.

"Do you know where Mr. Rochester is? How is he? What is he doing?" I asked.

"I don't know. The advert didn't say. He was probably a bad man," he said.

He took a letter out of his pocket and read it.

"No, he wasn't," I said.

"The girl was called Jane Eyre. I wasn't sure it was you until yesterday," Mr. St. John Rivers said.

"Where is the lawyer?" I asked.

"He is in London. You haven't asked what he wants you for," he replied.

"Well?" I asked.

"Your uncle is dead. You now own everything he did. You are rich now," he said.

"I am rich?" I was very surprised.

"Yes. You must go to London to see the lawyer, but then all the money and houses are yours. Twenty thousand pounds," he replied. I didn't know what to say.

"Wait, why did you tell me this?" I asked.

"I was named after you. I am St. John Eyre Rivers," he replied.

"You are my cousin?" I asked.

"Oh! How happy I am!" I cried.

"You are happy we are cousins, but not that you are rich?" he laughed at me.

"I have a family that I like! Of course, I am happy. Write to Mary and Diana. Tell them to come home. We will share the money, five thousand pounds each," I said.

"You don't need to give us your money. We are your family. You don't know what twenty thousand pounds can do for you," Mr. Rivers said.

"I don't care. I don't want to get married. I want my family to be taken care of," I said.

"We will have to close the school," he said.

"No, I will teach until a new teacher comes," I replied. He shook my hand and went home.

It was almost Christmas when the money had been given to all of us and we were all settled. I lived at Marsh End with Mary and Diana.

St. John lived by his church. He didn't spend much time at Marsh End. He liked being a vicar. Mary and Diana asked, "Does he still want to be a missionary?"

"He does. He is going next year," I replied.

"What about Miss Oliver?" Mary asked.

"She is marrying someone else."

After Christmas, Mary, Diana and I went back to learning. There was a new teacher at the school. I went to visit the school once a week. St. John asked me to give up learning German and learn Hindustani instead. I agreed. St. John taught me. I wanted to make him happy. I hadn't forgotten Mr. Rochester though. I couldn't forget him. I still loved him and wanted to be with him.

I wrote to Mrs. Fairfax to try to find out how he was. I got no reply. St. John pushed me to be better at Hindustani. I never thought of saying no to him. I couldn't say no to him. I waited for a letter from Mrs. Fairfax every day. When a letter came for me, I was very happy. But it was a letter from the lawyer. I was so upset I cried. St. John tried to calm me.

We went for a walk together. We sat looking at a small waterfall on the moor.

"Jane, I want you to come with me to India. I want you to marry me," he said. I knew he didn't love me. I could go to India and help him, but I knew I couldn't be his wife.

"No, I can't marry you, but I will go with you to India," I replied.

"But if you come to India, then you have to marry me," he said.

We went for a walk together.
We sat looking at a small waterfall on the moor.

"No, I won't," I said. St. John was angry with me.

Later, he didn't say goodnight to me. I asked him to forgive me. He said he would, but he wasn't my friend anymore. It was not nice living at Marsh End with him for the next few weeks. He was cold to me all the time.

Diana asked me what had happened and I explained what had happened. St. John went away for a week. When he came back, he asked me to marry him again. I said no and he was even angrier than before.

"You won't marry me because you love Mr. Rochester!" he cried. It was true.

He went away again for two weeks. When he came back, he was nice to me again. He was going to London to get ready to leave for India. He asked me to marry him again.

He acted like he loved me. He talked to me gently. He hugged me and I felt like I was ready to marry him. He told me to pray.

"I have been praying that you will marry me," he told me.

"I will pray about it," I told him. I closed my eyes. I heard Mr. Rochester's voice. It was calling me. I ran out of the house looking for him. There was no one there, just the dark on the moor.

I went to bed and locked the door. I prayed about Mr. Rochester and St. John. Then I went to sleep.

Chapter 10

St. John left the next morning. He put a letter under my door. I still didn't know what to do. Diana didn't think I should go. If I was going to go to India and marry St. John, there was only one person that was stopping me.

Mrs. Fairfax hadn't written back to me. I decided to go to Thornfield and find out what had happened. I told Mary and Diana what I was doing. I told them, "I will be gone for no more than four days."

"On your own?" they asked.

"Yes, I need to go and find out about a friend," I replied. It took two days to take a coach to Thornfield. I got out of the coach two miles from Thornfield and walked across the fields. I was sure that Mr. Rochester was in Europe. I didn't think that he had stayed at Thornfield after I left.

I almost ran down the last part of my journey. I wanted to see Thornfield again. I saw the trees I knew very well, and the hills and the meadows. I thought about the house. I knew I would see it soon. I was so happy to be there. I looked and there was no house. There were ruins in its place. It was like a horrible dream.

The garden was no longer beautiful. It was so quiet. I went to the ruins. A fire had destroyed Thornfield. I thought about how the fire had happened. There was no one there to ask what had happened. There was no sign to tell me either.

I went to the church to find out what had happened.

“Mr. Rochester is alive. The fire happened last autumn. It started in the middle of the night. I saw it from here. There was a mad woman in the house. She started the fire. She was Mr. Rochester’s wife. She was even madder because Mr. Rochester fell in love with a governess. He wanted to marry her. Mrs. Rochester set fire to her room. Mr. Rochester was very angry because he lost the girl he loved so he sent everyone away. He stayed at the hall. He was waiting for the girl to come back. He tried to save Mrs. Rochester from the fire, but she jumped off the roof. She is dead. Mr. Rochester is now blind. The house fell on him. He was pulled out and saved. He lost his hand as well,” the vicar said.

“Where is he?” I asked.

“At his other house. It is in the middle of the woods. Thirty miles from here,” he replied.

“Do you have a carriage that can take me there? If you can do it today, I will pay you twice,” I said.

The garden was no longer beautiful.
It was so quiet. I went to the ruins.

I got to the house before dark. It was a very lonely house. There were no flowers and it was dark in the trees. The door to the house opened. My Mr. Edward Rochester stood there. It was a year since I last saw him. I nearly called out to him. He came out of the house slowly. He walked with his hand out in front of him. He felt around until a servant came out to take him in.

I waited until the door closed. Then I went forward and knocked on the door.

"Hello Mary, how are you?" I said to the maid who opened the door. She looked at me like I was a ghost. My bags were brought into the house. The bell rang. Mary went to answer it. When she came back, she told me that he had asked for candles and water.

"I will take them to him," I said.

I went into the room. Mr. Rochester was sitting by the fire. Pilot lay in front of it. The dog jumped up at me.

"Lie down," Mr. Rochester said to the dog. I put down the tray and patted the dog. "Give me the water, Mary," Mr. Rochester said.

I gave the water to him. Pilot barked.

"What is the matter?" he asked.

"Down, Pilot," I said. Mr. Rochester turned his head towards me.

"Mary?" he asked.

He pulled his hand away and then wrapped it around me.
"Jane, is it you?" he asked.

"Mary is in the kitchen," I replied.

"Who is there?" he asked. He was nervous.

"Pilot knows me. The servants know me too," I said.

"I am going mad," he replied.

"No, you're not," I told him.

"Where are you?" he asked. I took his hand in both of mine. He pulled his hand away and then wrapped it around me. "Jane, is it you?" he asked.

“Yes, I have come back to you,” I said. He repeated my name over and over again.

“I dreamed that you would come back, and that you would tell me that you loved me, and that you would never leave me,” he said.

“I never will,” I replied. He kissed me. I told him what had happened since we were last together. He was quiet. I was worried that he wanted me to leave. I tried to get up.

“No, Jane, you can’t go,” he said.

“I will stay with you. I already said I would,” I replied.

“Staying is not good enough for you. You should be married. But I am not a man now,” he said.

“You are still a man,” I replied.

“I am scared that you will not be here when I wake up tomorrow,” he told me. I teased him until it was time for bed.

The next morning, I heard him asking for me. I had breakfast with him. I told him about St. John and Marsh End. He asked me many questions about St. John. I teased him with my answers. I told him that St. John had asked me to marry him.

“Leave me. Go and marry Rivers,” he told me.

“Make me. I will not leave unless you do,” I replied.

“Go, be with the husband that you have chosen,” he said.

“I am already there,” I replied.

“You will marry a poor blind man?” he asked.

“Yes,” I said.

“Really?” he asked.

“Yes,” I said. I told him that I heard him calling out to me. He told me that he had called for me exactly when I had heard him.

I married him. It was a quiet wedding. I told Mary when we got back to the house. I wrote to Mary, Diana and St. John. I told them I was now Mrs. Rochester, not Jane Eyre. Diana and Mary both came to meet Mr. Rochester.

I married him. It was a quiet wedding.

St. John never wrote back to me. Miss Varens came back to live with us. After two years of marriage, Mr. Rochester started to see again. Diana and Mary got married. Their husbands love them both as my husband loves me.

St. John went to India. He is still there. He is a good missionary and works hard. He will never get married. He is married to his work.

I am happy living with Mr. Rochester. We have been married for ten years. Mrs. Fairfax went to live with her family when Thornfield was lost. She is a **distant** cousin of Mr Rochester. She is happy in her new life. Miss Varens went to a good school and came back to see us in the holidays.

I was not happy when I was a girl called Jane Eyre. I am happy as a woman called Jane Rochester.

distant (adj) not closely related

GLOSSARY

abandon (v) to leave and never come back to someone/something

advert (n) advertisement, something (e.g. picture, film) shown to people to help sell a product

bring up (phrasal verb) to take care of a child and teach him or her how to behave

charity (n) an institution or organisation that helps people in need

clergyman (n) a male priest

cloak (n) a piece of clothing used as a coat

come off well (idiom) to be successful, to have a good result in a competition, fight, etc.

confused (adj) unable to understand or think clearly

distant (adj) not closely related

duel (n) a fight between two people

falling-out (n) a serious argument, a quarrel

forehead (n) the part of the face above the eyes

fortune teller (n) someone who tells you what will happen to you in the future

go by (phrasal verb) to pass (time)

governess (n) a woman who lives with a family and is paid to teach their child in their home

grip (v) to hold something tightly

impressed (adj) if you are impressed by something, you are strongly affected by it because it is so good and interesting

in a knot (phrase) twisted together (e.g. hair, string, shoelaces)

in charge of (phrase) responsible for, being in control of

knock someone down (phrasal verb) to hit someone and make them fall

lead (v) to show the way to someone

leap (v) to jump, to spring

modest (adj) a modest person doesn't talk too much about themselves or their abilities and doesn't show or feel great pride

moor (n) an open area of land that is not good for farming

nod (v) to move your head up and down as a way of showing agreement, understanding or approval

parlour (n) a room for guests (reception, lounge, waiting room)

peaceful (adj) quiet and calm, not liking violence; pleasant

put out (phrasal verb) to extinguish, to cause (e.g. fire) to stop burning

reply (v) to answer

selfish (adj) if you are selfish, you care only for yourself, not others

sermon (n) a speech about a religious subject or a moral topic

sit still (idiom) to sit without moving around

snarl (v) to speak in an angry way

sprain (v) to injure (e.g. ankle, knee) by twisting it in sudden and painful way

stool (n) a seat without back or arms

tease (v) to make fun of

tell somebody off (phrasal verb) to speak in an angry way to someone for doing something wrong

torture (n) something that gives you pain

tremble (v) to shake

turn against (phrasal verb) to stop being friendly to someone, to be their enemy

veil (n) a piece of cloth that women wear to cover their head and shoulders

vicar (n) a priest

ward (n) a child who lives under the protection of a guardian

whisk (v) to move someone or something to another place very quickly

whisper (v) to speak very softly or quietly

yell (v) to shout loudly because you are angry

ACTIVITIES

COMPREHENSION CHECK

Test 1

Are the following sentences TRUE (T) or FALSE (F)?

1. Elizia, John and Georgina were Jane's cousins. T / F

2. Miss Miller was the headmistress of Lowood School. T / F

3. Jane was hired as a governess for Miss Varens. T / F

4. Mr. Rochester didn't like children. T / F

5. Blanche thought she was going to marry Mr. Mason. T / F

6. John Reed died before Mrs. Reed. T / F

7. Grace was the one trying to kill Mr. Rochester. T / F

8. The house Diana and Mary River lived in was called Marsh End. T / F

9. Jane agreed to marry St. John Rivers and go to India. T / F

10. St. John Rivers got married to Miss Oliver. T / F

Test 1

Match the sentences.

Beginnings	Endings
1. I kissed her cheek and	a. so we had better clothes and food.
2. I have ordered a special lunch	b. remember what she wanted to say.
3. Lots of rich people gave money to the school	c. like the rest of her family.
4. I sat down and Miss Varens was	d. I felt better than I ever had before.
5. When she had finished, I saw her hand	e. here when I wake up tomorrow.
6. She wanted to talk to me, but she couldn't	f. about my life until Thornfield.
7. She is a witch and mad,	g. and I explained what had happened.
8. I told Mr. St. John Rivers	h. told to go and play with the dog.
9. Diana asked me what had happened	i. of bread and cheese for everyone.
10. I am scared that you will not be	j. and knew who the woman was.

Test 3

Who said this in the story? *Jane, Mr Rochester, Mrs. Reed, Helen, Mrs. Fairfax, St. John Rivers*

1. "Mr. Brocklehurst, will you take her to Lowood School or not

   ....

2. "Don't worry, nobody believes Mr. Brocklehurst."

   ....

3. "Come meet Jane Eyre, she is your new governess."

   ....

4. "His sad thoughts make his mood change very quickly."

   ....

5. "You are cold, you are sick and you are silly."

   ....

6. "I have found you one in Ireland. You will like it there."

   ....

7. "Yes. I don't want to talk. I need water."

   ....

8. "You will have a home and teach the girls from the village."

   ....

9. "No, I will teach until a new teacher comes."

   ....

10. "Leave me. Go and marry Rivers."

   ....

Test 4

Answer the questions below.

1. What is the name of the doctor that comes to see Jane at Gateshead Hall?
2. What did Miss Temple give Jane and Helen to eat with their tea?
3. Where does Miss Varens say that Mr. Rochester is when Jane arrives?
4. What was the name of Miss Varens' mother?
5. Why did Mr. Mason come to Thornfield?
6. What is Mr. Rochester's first name?
7. Who took Jane in after she left Thornfield?
8. What was the name of the woman that St. John Rivers was in love with?
9. Who was named after Jane?
10. What was the name of Mr. Rochester's dog?

Test 5

Put the list in order by entering the numbers 1 to 10 in the gaps below.

---

a. ___ Jane walked to the village and a man fell off his horse.

b. ___ Jane returned to Mr. Rochester.

c. ___ Mr. Rochester asked Jane to marry him.

d. ___ Bessie locked Jane in the red room.

e. ___ Jane painted a portrait of Miss Oliver.

f. ___ Jane saved Mr. Rochester from being burned alive in his bed.

g. ___ Mr. Rochester and Jane's wedding was interrupted by Mr. Mason

h. ___ Helen died as Jane slept next to her.

i. ___ Jane inherited her uncle's money.

j. ___ Mr. Rochester dressed up as a fortune teller.

GRAMMAR CHECK

Test 1

Complete the sentences with the correct preposition.

1. She was .... a lot of pain after her friend left her.
2. He suggested that we should leave .... sunset as it would be cooler to drive then.
3. He rang the fire brigade as soon as he realised that the house was .... fire.
4. Mr. Rochester fought a duel .... the man his wife was with.
5. Why are you staring .... me like that?
6. She told me that she would be here .... a minute but half an hour has passed and she is not here yet.
7. I want you to be happy and successful and I don't want to let anything stand .... your way.
8. I can't understand you. Stop talking .... riddles!
9. Did they find out who set fire .... the house?
10. She is .... no mood for jokes now. You'd better leave her alone for a while.

Test 2

Complete the sentences with *while, during* **or** *for.*

1. We visited many places .... our holiday.
2. David has been learning Spanish .... three years, but he still can't speak it very well.
3. The pilot announced that we should remain seated .... the flight.
4. Their house was broken into .... they were on holiday.
5. I am looking forward to playing tennis this Sunday as I haven't played it .... two years.
6. The Prime Minister talked about various issues .... his speech.
7. My neighbour looked after my cat .... I was on vacation.
8. He wanted to sit in a cafe and wait for us .... we were shopping.
9. He has been playing for Arsenal .... eight years, but he will be transfered to Chelsea next month.
10. Millions of people died .... the Second World War.

VOCABULARY CHECK

Test 1

Fill in the blanks with the words below.

forehead	**abandon**	**sermon**	**impressed**	**sprained**
modest	**torture**	**whispering**	**peaceful**	**teased**

1. We were all .... by his performance during the game.

2. The footballer was left with 10 stiches in his .... after he bumped into the goal post during the match.

3. The prisoner died due to brutal .... in prison.

4. There was so much snow on the road that drivers had to .... their vehicles and continue their journey on foot.

5. Their neighbourhood is so .... and quiet. Also, its people are very friendly and kind.

6. She is a very .... woman. She doesn't like boasting about her achievements.

7. His classmates .... him because he was short.

8. I couldn't hear what they were talking about because they were ....

9. While he was walking home, he fell and .... his ankle.

10. There were only a few people during the .... at the church.

Test-2

Match the definitions (1-10) on the right with the words (a-j) on the left.

a. ___selfish	1. to speak in an angry way
b. ___grip	2. a male priest
c. ___vicar	3. to make fun of
d. ___leap	4. caring only for yourself, not others
e. ___duel	5. to hold something tightly
f. ___falling-out	6. to jump
g. ___distant	7. a priest
h. ___clergyman	8. a fight between two people
i. ___tease	9. not closely related
j. ___snarl	10. a serious argument

ANSWER KEY

COMPREHENSION CHECK

Test 1

1.	True
2.	False
3.	True
4.	True
5.	False
6.	True
7.	False
8.	True
9.	False
10.	False

Test 2

1.	d
2.	i
3.	a
4.	h
5.	j
6.	b
7.	c
8.	f
9.	g
10.	e

Test 3

1. Mrs. Reed
2. Helen
3. Mrs. Fairfax
4. Mrs. Fairfax
5. Mr. Rochester/the Fortune Teller
6. Mr. Rochester
7. Jane Eyre
8. St. John Rivers
9. Jane Eyre
10. Mr. Rochester

Test 4

1. Mr. Lloyd
2. Seed cake
3. France
4. Celine
5. To see his sister and Mr. Rochester
6. Edward
7. Mr. St. John Rivers and his sisters
8. Miss Oliver
9. St. John Rivers
10. Pilot

Test 5

a.	3
b.	10
c.	6
d.	1
e.	8
f.	4
g.	7
h.	2
i.	9
j.	5

GRAMMAR CHECK

Test 1	Test 2
1. in	1. during
2. at	2. for
3. on	3. during
4. against	4. while
5. at	5. for
6. in	6. during
7. in	7. while
8. in	8. while
9. to	9. for
10. in	10. during

VOCABULARY CHECK

Test 1	Test 2
1. impressed	a. 4
2. forehead	b. 5
3. torure	c. 7
4. abandon	d. 6
5. peaceful	e. 8
6. modest	f. 10
7. teased	g. 9
8. whispering	h. 2
9. sprained	i. 3
10. sermon	j. 1